Body Talk

Pump It Up

RESPIRATION AND CIRCULATION

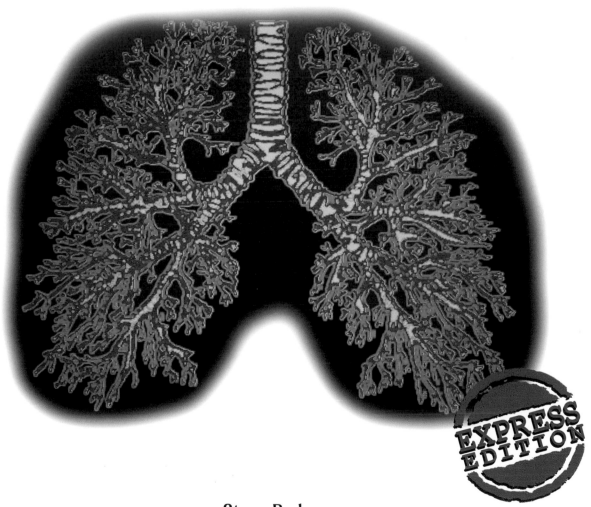

EXPRESS EDITION

Steve Parker

Raintree

www.raintreepublishers.co.uk
Visit our website to find out more information about **Raintree** books.

To order:
☎ Phone 44 (0) 1865 888113
▤ Send a fax to 44 (0) 1865 314091
▢ Visit the Raintree bookshop at **www.raintreepublishers.co.uk**
to browse our catalogue and order online.

First published in Great Britain by Raintree, Halley Court, Jordan Hill, Oxford, OX2 8EJ, part of Harcourt Education.
Raintree is a registered trademark of Harcourt Education Ltd.

Editorial: Kathryn Walker, Melanie Waldron, Rosie Gordon, and Megan Cotugno
Design: Philippa Jenkins, Lucy Owen, John Walker, and Rob Norridge
Illustrations: Darren Linguard and Jeff Edwards
Picture Research: Mica Brancic and Ginny Stroud-Lewis
Production: Chloe Bloom
Originated by Modern Age Repro
Printed and bound in China by South China Printing Company

10 digit ISBN 1 406 20418 8 (hardback)
13 digit ISBN 978 1 4062 0418 6 (hardback)
11 10 09 08 07

10 digit ISBN 1 406 20425 0 (paperback)
13 digit ISBN 978 1 4062 0425 4 (paperback)
10 09 08 07

British Library Cataloguing in Publication Data
Parker, Steve
Pump it up! : respiration and circulation. - (Body talk)
1.Cardiovascular system - Juvenile literature
2.Respiration
- Juvenile literature
I.Title
612.1
A full catalogue record for this book is available from the British Library.

This levelled text is a version of *Freestyle: Body Talk: Pump It Up*

Acknowledgements
The publishers would like to thank the following for permission to reproduce photographs: Alamy Images p. 35 (ImageState),p. 18-19 (Redferns Music Picture Library); Corbis pp. 4-5, 7, 16-17, 22-23, 39; p. 26 (Zefa/ Niven), 30-31 (Annie Griffiths Belt), p. 12 (Christian Liewig), pp. 26-27 (Don Mason), p. 28 (Lester Lefkowitz), pp. 36-37 (Michael & Patricia Fogden), p. 9 (Reuters), p. 14 (Saba/Marc Asnin), pp. 40-41 (Stephanie Maze); Getty pp. 20, 32-33; 21 (Digital Vision), pp. 37, 40 (PhotoDisc), p. 8 (Stone); Harcourt Education Ltd/Tudor Photography pp. 6-7; Richard Smith p. 41; Science Photo Library pp. 28-29; pp. 10-11 (Alfred Pasieka), pp. 38-39 (Andrew Syred); pp. 23, 24-25, 42-43 (BSIP), p. 25 (CNRI), p. 18 (David M Martin, MD), pp. 12-13, 42-43 (Eye of Science), pp. 42-43 (Herve Conge, ISM), p. 10 (J. L. Carson, Custom Medical Stock, Photo), p. 31 (Mark Thomas), p. 11 (Simon Fraser), p. 9 (Steve Vowles), pp. 34-35 (Susumu Nishinaga), pp. 14-15 (Tony McConnell). Cover photograph reproduced with permission of Getty Images/ Reportage / Daniel Berehulak.

The author and publisher would like to thank Ann Fullick for her assistance in the preparation of this book.

Dedicated to the memory of Lucy Owen

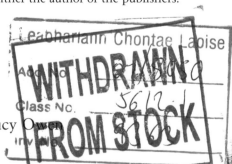

Contents

Any words appearing in the text in bold, **like this,** are explained in the glossary. You can also look out for them in 'Body language' at the bottom of each page.

Take a deep breath

Do you remember the last time you got really out of breath? Maybe it was after running. Perhaps you had been playing some sport.

Bursting lungs, pounding heart

When you are out of breath you try to take in more air. Sometimes it feels as if your lungs might burst. Your heart thumps hard and fast.

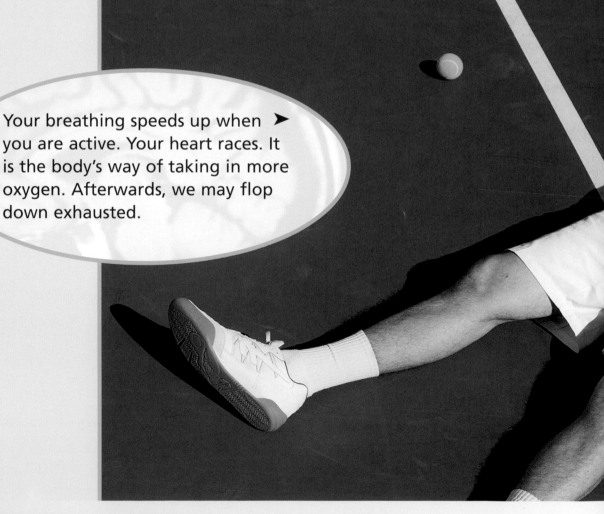

Your breathing speeds up when ➤ you are active. Your heart races. It is the body's way of taking in more oxygen. Afterwards, we may flop down exhausted.

The breathing system

You use your **respiratory system** to breathe. This is a set of parts inside your body. It includes your nose. It also includes the lungs in your chest.

These parts work together. They take oxygen from the air. They pass it into your blood.

They also push out **carbon dioxide**. You don't need this gas. Your body produces carbon dioxide as it works.

The need to breathe

We always need to breathe. We need to get oxygen. Some people can hold their breath for a long time. But they will feel a great urge to breathe again.

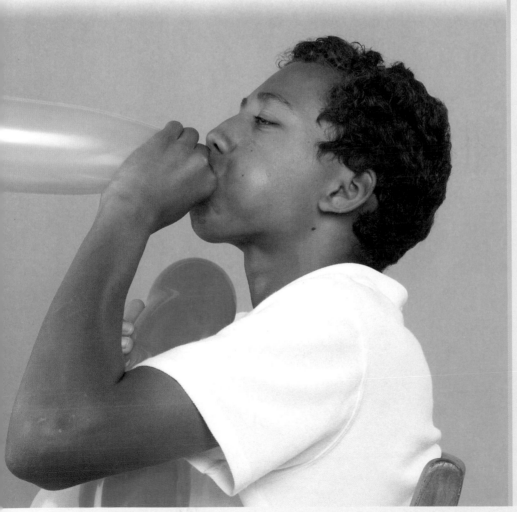

7

Cleaning up the air

You usually breathe in through your nose. Inside your nostrils you have small hairs. These trap floating dust and dirt.

Your nose is also lined with a sticky substance. This is **mucus** (snot). It traps more dust and germs.

In these ways the nose cleans the air. It cleans the air as it travels to your lungs.

Changing the air

The mucus inside your nose is moist. It makes the air moist as it passes through.

Sticky and slimy

The inside of your nose makes a cupful of mucus each day. Some illnesses make it produce much more mucus. This happens if we catch a cold.

◄ A sneeze blasts out millions of tiny drops of mucus. It is best to catch them in a tissue. This can stop other people breathing them in.

mucus   sticky fluid in various body parts

Also, there are lots of small **blood vessels** in the nose. These are tiny tubes that carry warm blood. They warm up the cold air.

So your nose makes air clean, warm, and moist. This is just how your lungs like it to be.

◄ Top sports people need to get lots of air into their lungs. Some wear sticky patches on their noses. These help keep the airways there wide open.

blood vessels   tubes that carry blood

Down, down, down

You breathe in. Air goes down your throat. Then it moves down your windpipe. In your chest, the windpipe branches into two tubes.

These tubes are called **bronchi** tubes. One leads to the right lung. The other leads to the left lung.

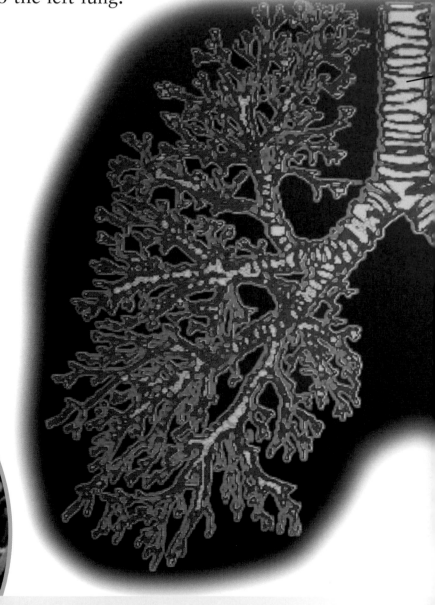

Clearing your throat

The main airways are lined with sticky **mucus**. They are also lined with millions of tiny hairs (below). These are called **cilia**. Mucus traps germs. Cilia move the mucus up. We cough it up. Then we swallow it or spit it out.

cilia

mucus

cilia microscopic "hairs" on the cells of some body parts. Cilia wave backwards and forwards.

Thinner, shorter

Each of the bronchi splits into two smaller tubes. Each of these tubes splits again. This happens about 15 times. The tubes keep getting thinner and shorter. They are called **bronchioles**. Finally the air is deep inside the lungs.

Warning – don't smoke

Smoking tobacco kills the tiny cilia hairs in the airways (see page 10). Without the cilia, mucus collects in your lungs. This causes disease.

windpipe

◄ The airways in your chest look like an upside-down tree. The windpipe is like the trunk. The large bronchi are like main branches. Bronchioles are the twigs.

bronchiole

11

Millions of micro-bubbles

Air reaches the deepest parts of your lungs. Then it flows into millions of tiny "caves". These are called **alveoli**. Alveoli are like air bubbles. They make the lungs feel like sponge.

There is a net of **capillaries** around each alveolus. Capillaries are the tiniest tubes that carry blood.

Tiny bubbles

The lungs' alveoli (air bubbles) are tiny. You need a microscope to see them.

alveolus

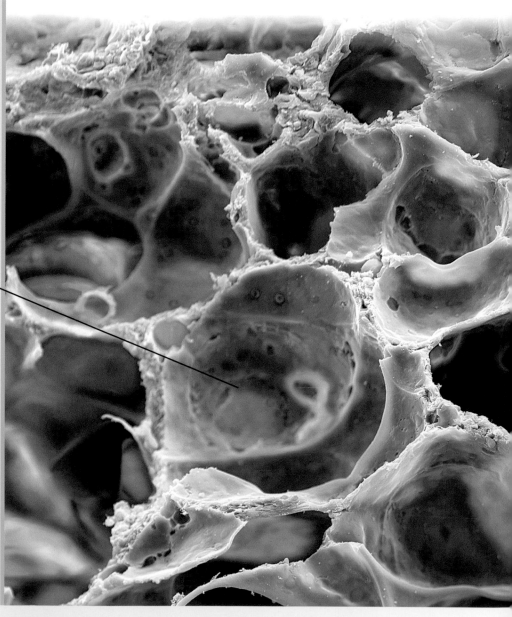

Body language   alveoli   tiny air spaces in the lungs. A single space is called an alveolus.

Oxygen in

Alveoli are filled with air. This is where blood gets **oxygen**. The blood in the capillaries carries it through your body.

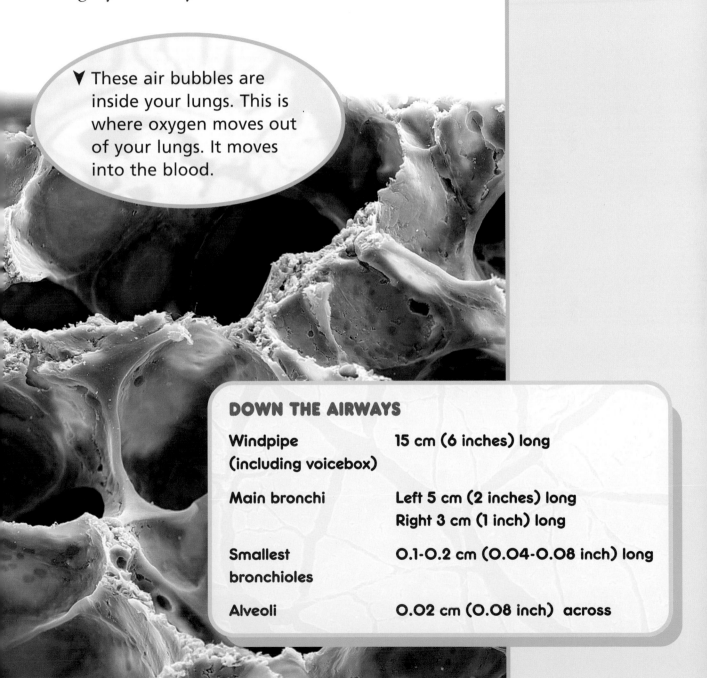

▼ These air bubbles are inside your lungs. This is where oxygen moves out of your lungs. It moves into the blood.

DOWN THE AIRWAYS

Windpipe (including voicebox)	15 cm (6 inches) long
Main bronchi	Left 5 cm (2 inches) long Right 3 cm (1 inch) long
Smallest bronchioles	0.1-0.2 cm (0.04-0.08 inch) long
Alveoli	0.02 cm (0.08 inch) across

capillaries tiniest blood vessels

Straight swap

You breathe out the same amount of air you breathe in. But your body has used up **oxygen** from the breathed-in air. So what replaces it in the air you breathe out?

The answer is **carbon dioxide**. Your body produces this gas as it works. But your body doesn't need it.

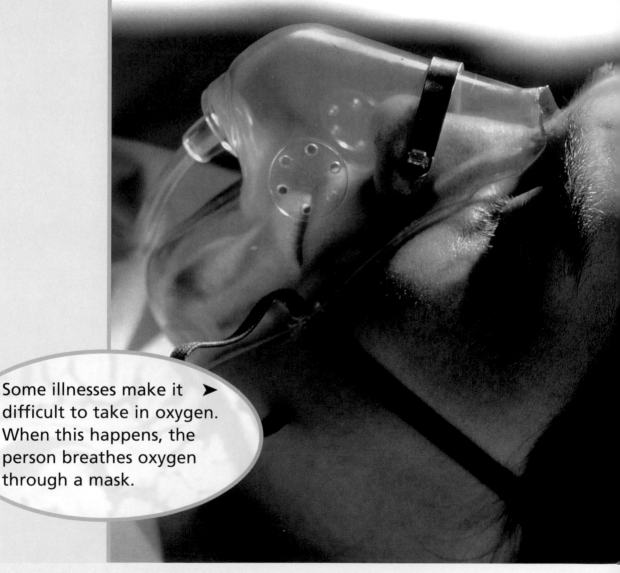

Some illnesses make it ➤ difficult to take in oxygen. When this happens, the person breathes oxygen through a mask.

carbon dioxide   waste gas made by the body and breathed out

One in, one out

Blood collects carbon dioxide from around the body. It carries this gas to the lungs.

In the lungs carbon dioxide leaves the blood. At the same time, oxygen moves into the blood.

Back again

You breathe air in. Almost straight away you are ready to breathe out air. This air now has less oxygen. Instead it has more carbon dioxide. The stale air flows back up the airways. Then it leaves the body.

Thin walls

The walls of an **alveolus** (below) are extremely thin. So are the walls of the **capillary**. This makes it easy for oxygen to pass into the blood.

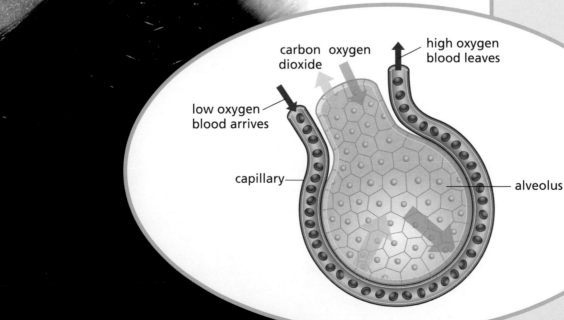

carbon dioxide

oxygen

high oxygen blood leaves

low oxygen blood arrives

capillary

alveolus

Breathing and talking

All body movements are made with muscles. Breathing uses two main sets of muscles. The first is a sheet of muscle under your lungs. This is the **diaphragm**. The second set is between your ribs. They are called **intercostals** (see diagram below).

Breathing in

The diaphragm looks like an upside-down bowl. But it becomes flatter when you breathe in. This stretches the lungs down. They get bigger. Air fills them up.

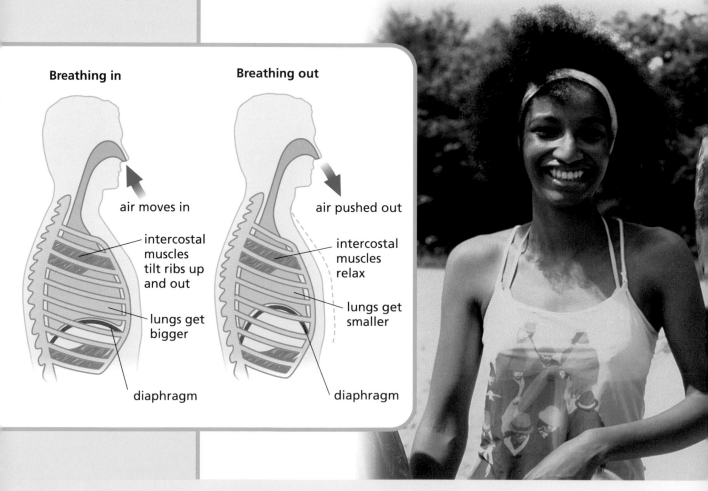

Breathing in

air moves in

intercostal muscles tilt ribs up and out

lungs get bigger

diaphragm

Breathing out

air pushed out

intercostal muscles relax

lungs get smaller

diaphragm

diaphragm   large sheet of muscle under the lungs that helps you breathe

Intercostal muscles push the ribs up and out. This happens when you breathe in. It stretches the lungs forwards. They get bigger. So air moves in.

Out again

To breathe out, the breathing muscles relax. The lungs spring back to their smaller size. This pushes out air.

◄ To blow out hard we use our normal breathing muscles. But we also use extra muscles in our upper and lower body.

intercostals   strap-like muscles between each pair of ribs

"Hello, how are you?"

You use your **respiratory** (breathing) **system** to talk. You use it to make other noises too. Sounds come from inside your neck. They come from your **larynx**. This is also called your voicebox.

Box of tricks

Inside the voicebox are two flaps. These are called **vocal cords**. When you breathe normally, air passes through a gap between the flaps.

Vocal cords

When we are breathing normally, the vocal cords are apart (below).

vocal cords

If you want to speak, muscles pull the flaps almost together. Air then has to pass through a narrow gap. This makes the flaps vibrate. The vibrations make the sound of your voice.

Shaping the sounds

The sounds from your vocal cords are quiet. Other parts of your body work to make them louder. Your throat, mouth, and nose do this. So do your tongue and lips. Together, they change the sounds into clear words.

Out, out, out ...
The voicebox works when air is breathed out. Try to speak while breathing in. It's very difficult!

◄ We can change our voice in many ways. Breathing out harder makes it louder.

vocal cords two parts inside the voicebox

Hardworking heart

**Heart ache,
heart break**
We often talk
about the heart
when we discuss
strong feelings.
Feelings are
actually in the
brain. But the
brain does make
the heart beat
faster. It does this
when we are
excited or
stressed.

Your heart has to be the hardest-working part
of your body. It pumps every second of your life.
It sends blood round and round your body.

Blood carries hundreds of substances to every part
of you. It carries **oxygen**. It also carries **nutrients**.
Nutrients come from food. Your body needs them
to work properly.

Where is the heart?

The heart is about the size of a clenched fist. It is
behind the breastbone (see picture page 21). It is
surrounded by the two lungs.

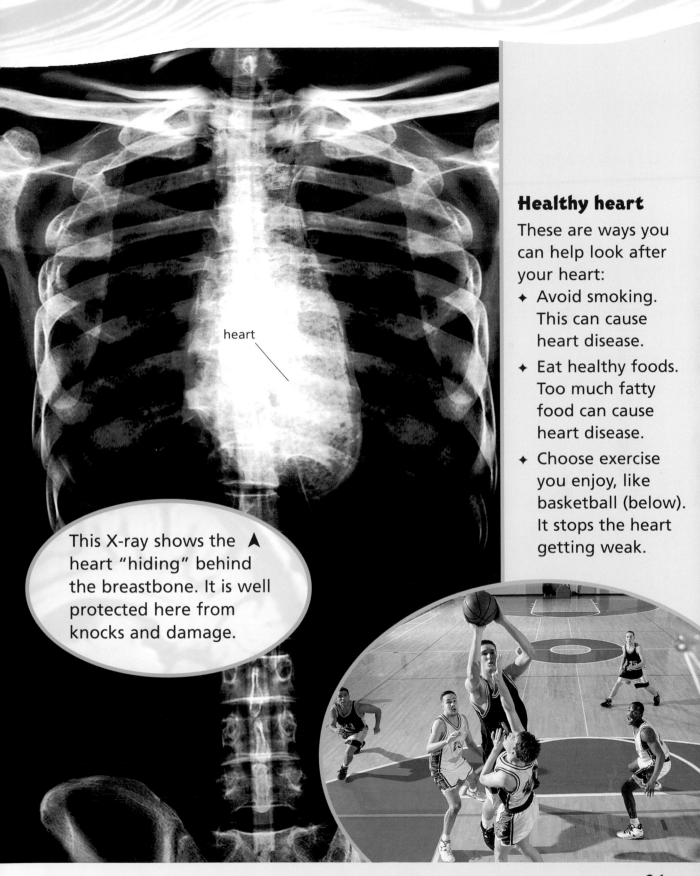

heart

This X-ray shows the ▲ heart "hiding" behind the breastbone. It is well protected here from knocks and damage.

Healthy heart

These are ways you can help look after your heart:

✦ Avoid smoking. This can cause heart disease.

✦ Eat healthy foods. Too much fatty food can cause heart disease.

✦ Choose exercise you enjoy, like basketball (below). It stops the heart getting weak.

Left and right

The left side of the heart has thicker walls. It is more powerful than the right side. This is because it has to pump blood all around the body. The right side only pumps blood to the nearby lungs.

Two hearts in one

Your heart is not just one pump. It is two pumps. They sit side by side. We need two because blood travels along two routes.

One route is short. It is called the **pulmonary circulation**. It carries blood between the heart and lungs. Blood gets **oxygen** from the lungs. Then it returns to the heart.

All around the body

The blood leaves the heart again. This time it takes a much longer route. This is called the **systemic circulation**. It takes the blood all around the body. Blood carries oxygen. Your body needs this oxygen to stay alive.

Humans make many kinds ➤ of pumping machines. This oil pump may last 10 or 20 years. But some hearts keep pumping for more than 100 years!

pulmonary circulation   movement of blood from the heart to the lungs, then back to the heart

Non-stop muscle

The walls of the heart (above) are a special kind of muscle. This muscle doesn't get tired. Exercise helps keep it thick and strong.

systemic circulation movement of blood from the heart, through the body, then back to the heart

Heartbeat

You can easily hear a heart beat. You can hear it if you press your ear against someone's chest.

The heartbeat is the sound made by parts inside the heart. These parts are called **valves**. They make sure the blood keeps flowing the right way. The noise you hear is made when the valves snap shut.

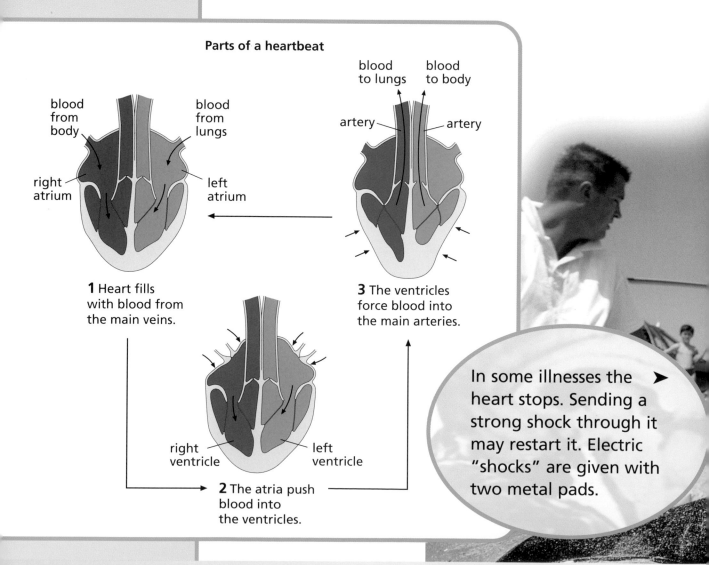

Parts of a heartbeat

blood from body

blood from lungs

right atrium

left atrium

1 Heart fills with blood from the main veins.

blood to lungs

blood to body

artery

artery

3 The ventricles force blood into the main arteries.

right ventricle

left ventricle

2 The atria push blood into the ventricles.

In some illnesses the heart stops. Sending a strong shock through it may restart it. Electric "shocks" are given with two metal pads.

atrium   small, upper pumping chamber of the heart

Upper and lower

The heart has two sides. Each side has two hollow chambers. The upper chamber is called the **atrium**. The lower chamber is the **ventricle** (see diagram, page 24).

On both sides, blood first comes into the atrium. The atrium squeezes blood into the ventricle. The ventricle then squeezes the blood out of the heart.

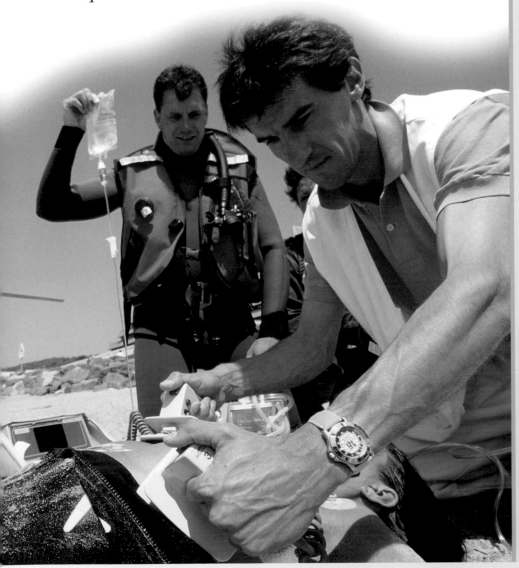

Heartbeats

Bigger animals usually have slower heartbeat rates. But their hearts are much bigger. A whale's heart is the size of a small car!

Beats per minute

Mouse	500
Cat	120
Human	70
Elephant	30
Great whale	10

ventricle   larger, lower pumping chamber of the heart

Hearing the heart

A doctor hears heartbeats through a listening tube. This is called a **stethoscope** (below). A doctor can hear how fast the heart is beating. A doctor can also hear if the heart is working properly.

Speed beat

Sometimes your muscles have to work really hard. This happens when you exercise or play sport. Then your muscles need lots of blood. The heart beats faster.

Other times the muscles aren't working hard. Then they need much less blood. The heartbeat is slower.

The heart's own blood supply

All body parts need blood. The heart has its own blood tubes. These tubes are called **coronary vessels**. They bring the heart blood that carries lots of **oxygen**. The heart needs this for its non-stop work.

coronary vessels tubes that carry blood to and from the heart walls

▼ Feeling scared or frightened can make the heart beat faster. This is the body getting ready for action. You may need to get away from danger.

27

Set the pace

You don't have to think about how fast your heart beats. You don't have to think about how strongly it beats. Your brain controls this. It does this in two main ways.

One way is by sending messages to the heart. The brain sends messages as signals. The signals pass along string-like parts. These are called **nerves**.

The other way is by sending messages to parts called the **adrenal glands**. These make a substance called **adrenalin**. Adrenalin makes the heart beat faster and harder.

Check your own heart rate

The heart squeezes out blood as it beats. This makes bulges, or pulsations, in the blood tubes. You can feel this in your wrist (see below).

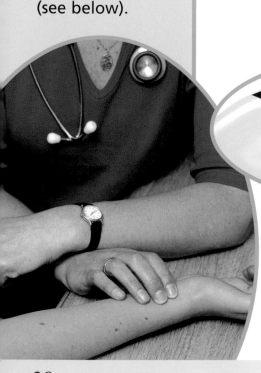

◄ Medical staff often check the pulse. They count how many pulsations there are in a minute.

nerves   string-like parts that carry messages around the body as tiny pulses of electricity

Pacemakers

The heart has a **pacemaker**. This is a patch in the upper right side of the heart.

The pacemaker makes the walls of the heart squeeze together. It makes them squeeze at the right time and speed. This keeps the blood pumping smoothly.

Heart facts

At rest
✦ Average number of heartbeats – 70 per minute

During exercise
✦ Average number of heartbeats – 150 per minute

Number of heartbeats
✦ Over 100,000 in one day
✦ Almost 40 million in one year
✦ Over 3 billion in an average lifetime.

▲ Sometimes a pacemaker goes wrong. Then doctors can put in a human-made pacemaker. It is joined by wires to the heart. It steadies the heartbeat.

Blood vessels

Blood reaches almost every tiny part of the body (see right). If you could join up all your blood vessels, they would go twice around the world!

Every city has a road network. Your body has a similar network. It is made of **blood vessels**. Blood vessels are tubes that carry blood around the body.

Big, small, big again

There are three main types of blood vessels. The first kind is **arteries**. They take blood from the heart.

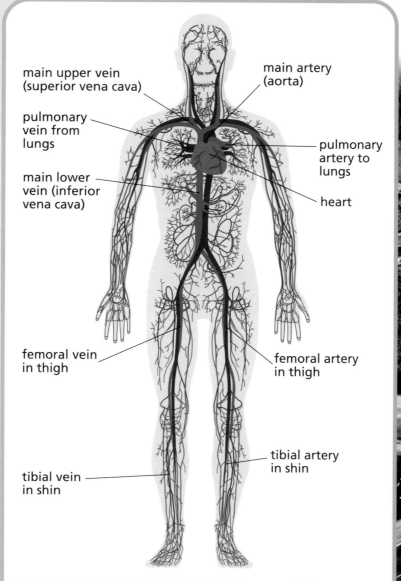

main upper vein (superior vena cava)

pulmonary vein from lungs

main lower vein (inferior vena cava)

main artery (aorta)

pulmonary artery to lungs

heart

femoral vein in thigh

femoral artery in thigh

tibial artery in shin

tibial vein in shin

oxygen gas that makes up one-fifth of air

Collecting the rubbish

At the same time, wastes move into the capillaries. Wastes are things the body doesn't need.

This delivery and collection only happens in capillaries. Other blood vessel walls are too thick.

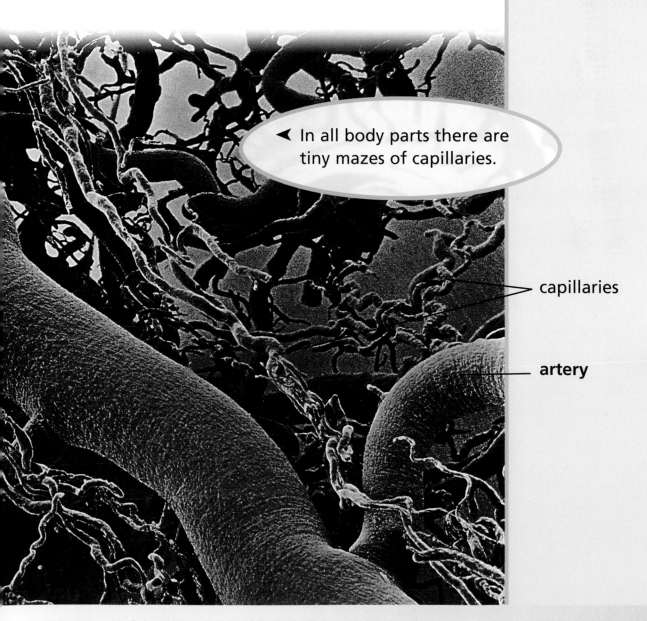

◄ In all body parts there are tiny mazes of capillaries.

capillaries

artery

Blood

Millions in a drop

One drop of blood the size of this "o" contains:

+ 25 million red blood cells
+ 25,000 white cells.

Blood carries supplies to your body **cells**. These supplies give you **energy**. They keep you healthy.

Blood spreads warmth to all your body parts. It collects wastes from your cells. Blood also helps your body fight germs.

What is in blood?

Slightly more than half your blood is a pale yellow liquid. This is called **plasma**. Plasma contains

A vampire bat laps up ➤ blood from big animals. The bat lives on blood alone. So blood must contain everything it needs to live.

nutrients (substances your body needs). These substances come from food. Slightly less than half your blood is **red blood cells**. These are the cells that carry **oxygen**.

About one-hundredth of your blood is **white blood cells**. White cells fight germs and disease. They also clean the blood. There are also other materials in the blood (see pages 42–43).

HOW MUCH BLOOD?

An average adult has about five litres (1 gallon) of blood. This is about equal to half a typical bucketful.

Save a life

Many people can save a life by giving blood. Blood is taken from an arm **vein**. This blood is stored (see below). It is put into people who have lost blood.

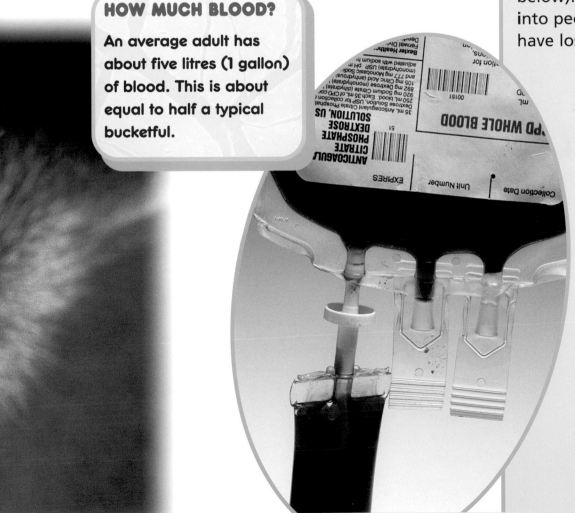

Grab and carry

Your blood is red because it contains **red blood cells**. You have billions of them.

Red cells have a special job. It is to carry **oxygen**. They gather oxygen from the lungs. This makes the cells bright red in colour.

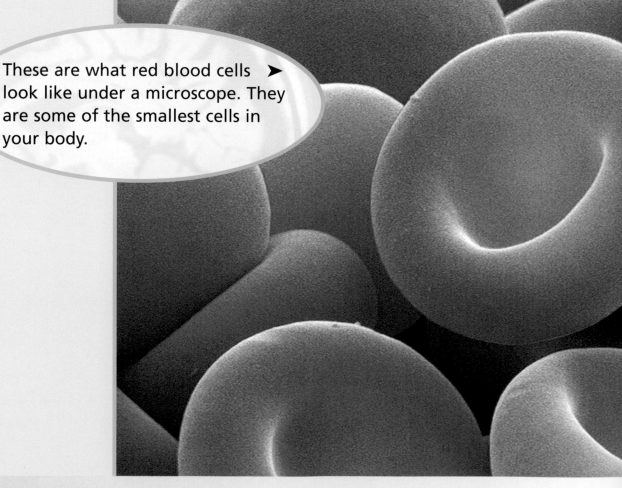

These are what red blood cells ➤ look like under a microscope. They are some of the smallest cells in your body.

red blood cells cells that carry oxygen around the body

Changing colour

Then blood sets off around your body. The red blood cells release oxygen. They release it to the cells that need it.

Red blood cells also take away **carbon dioxide** from body cells. The colour of red cells changes when they swap oxygen for carbon dioxide. They become a darker reddish-blue.

Look – red cells!

Sometimes we see "floaters". These look like tiny circles in front of our eyes. They may be red blood cells. These cells have escaped from the eye's **blood vessels**.

Why we need oxygen

Your lungs breathe. Your heart pumps. Your blood flows. This all happens to get **oxygen** to your body **cells**. But why do they need oxygen?

Blood cells need oxygen to get **energy**. We need energy to stay alive.

Energy powers our every move. It comes from our food. But we can only set it free if we have oxygen as well. ➤

energy   ability to cause changes and make things happen

Working together

Blood has many jobs. Clotting is just one of them. The blood's main job is to move all around the body. It must carry **oxygen** from the lungs. The heart pumps it through.

The breathing system and blood system work together to make this happen. Every second they breathe and pump to keep us alive.

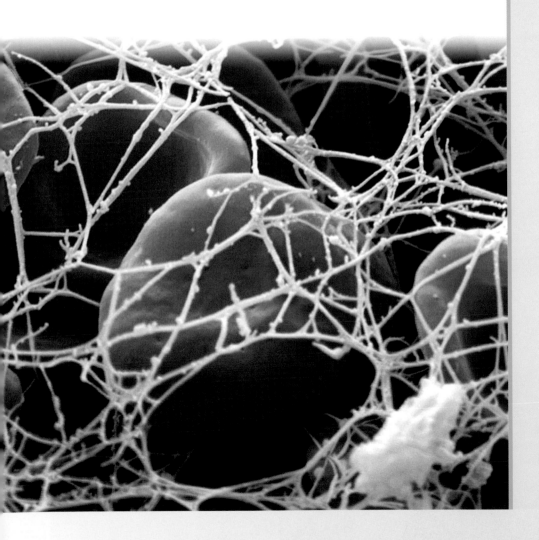

Find out more

Did you know?

◆ At rest, your heart pumps about 75 ml (2.5 fluid ounces) of blood in one heartbeat. In 15 minutes, it would pump enough blood to fill a bathtub.

◆ During exercise, your heart pumps more than 200 ml (7 fluid ounces) of blood in one heartbeat. It would take just three minutes to pump enough to fill a bathtub.

Books

First Human Body Encyclopedia, Penny Smith (Dorling Kindersley, 2005)

The Heart, Lungs and Blood, Steve Parker (Hodder Children's Books, 2003)

Heart Under the Microscope, Clive Gregory (Franklin Watts, 2001)

World Wide Web

The Internet can tell you more about your heart, lungs, and blood. You can use a search engine or search directory.

Type in keywords such as:

● heart
● respiratory system
● blood
● fitness and exercise
● circulatory system
● cells

Search tips

There are billions of pages on the Internet. It can be difficult to find what you are looking for.

These search skills will help you find useful websites more quickly:

- Know exactly what you want to find out about.
- Use two to six keywords in a search. Put the most important words first.
- Only use names of people, places, or things.

Where to search

Search engine
A search engine looks through millions of pages. It lists all the sites that match the words in the search box. You will find the best matches are at the top of the list, on the first page. Try **bbc.co.uk/search**

Search directory
A person instead of a computer has sorted a search directory. You can search by keyword or subject and browse through the different sites. It is like looking through books on a library shelf. Try **yahooligans.com**

Glossary

adrenal glands two glands above the kidneys. They make several hormones including adrenalin.

adrenalin hormone that gets the body ready for action

alveoli tiny air spaces in the lung. A single space is called an alveolus.

arteries larger blood vessels that carry blood away from the heart

arterioles smaller blood vessels that carry blood away from the heart

atrium small, upper pumping chamber of the heart

blood glucose sugar obtained when food is broken down. It is the body's main source of energy.

blood vessels tubes that carry blood. Arteries, capillaries, and veins are all blood vessels.

bronchi large air tubes that branch from the bottom of the windpipe. They carry air into the lungs.

bronchioles small tubes that take air from the large airways to the deepest parts of the lungs

capillaries tiniest blood vessels

carbon dioxide waste gas made by the body and breathed out

cells microscopic "building blocks" that make up all body parts

cilia microscopic "hairs" on the cells of some body parts. Cilia wave backwards and forwards.

clot lump of blood that seals a wound

clotting becoming thick and lumpy

contract become smaller or shorter. When a muscle contracts it pulls on the bones attached to it.

coronary vessels arteries and veins that carry blood to and from the heart walls

diaphragm large sheet of muscle under the lungs that helps you breathe

energy ability to cause changes and make things happen

intercostals strap-like muscles between each pair of ribs

larynx voicebox in the neck

mucus sticky fluid in various body parts. It gathers dust and germs, and it helps substances slip past easily.

nerves string-like parts that carry messages around the body as tiny pulses of electricity

nutrients useful substances in food that the body needs

oxygen gas that makes up one-fifth of air

pacemaker area in the upper right side of the heart. It controls the heartbeat.

plasma pale yellow liquid part of blood

platelets bits of cells that are needed in blood clotting

pulmonary circulation movement of blood from the heart to the lungs, then back to the heart

red blood cells cells that carry oxygen around the body

respiratory system body parts, such as the bronchi or nose, that take in air

stethoscope listening device for hearing body sounds

systemic circulation movement of blood from the heart, through the body, then back to the heart

valve device that controls the flow of a substance

vein large blood vessel that carries blood to the heart

ventricle larger, lower pumping chamber of the heart

venules small veins that collect blood from capillaries. They join up to form veins.

vocal cords two parts on either side of your larynx. They vibrate to make the sounds of your voice.

white blood cells pale cells in the blood. They clean blood and fight germs and disease.

Index

Titles in the *Freestyle Express: Body Talk* series include:

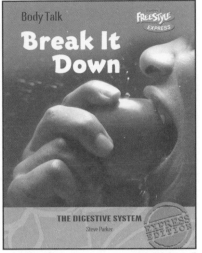

Hardback   1-406-20414-5

Hardback   1-406-20415-3

Hardback   1-406-20419-6

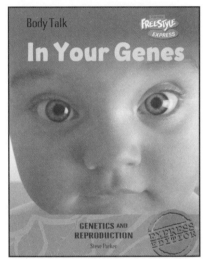

Hardback   1-406-20416-1

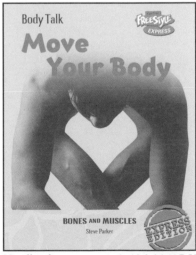

Hardback   1-406-20417-X

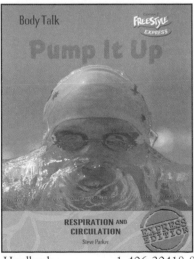

Hardback   1-406-20418-8

Find out about the other titles in this series on our website www.raintreepublishers.co.uk